BEING A MOM IS REALLY HARD

A MOTHER COMPARES THE BABY JOURNAL

TO HER OWN DIARY

by

Tanya Loosenort

Dedicated to Mom.   (Grandma Paige)

Look Mom, I did it! You always knew I could. You've always been my cheerleader, even though the stands were empty and I wasn't even playing a sport. I was just walking. Down the grocery aisle.

When the pimple took up the entirety of my face, you stood firm with an, "I don't see it, what are you talking about? Are those scones, what's a scone? I want one!"

I'm not saying you are the best Mom in the world. Everybody says that about their Mom. They're wrong. See what I did there?

Thank you. I love you.

8.8.2017

Baby Journal

I don't know how to tell you this Carebear, and maybe I shouldn't. But the

pen keeps moving and I love you. You need to know I love you.

8.8.2017

Tanya's Diary

[no entry]

5.26.2016

Baby Journal

[no entry]

5.26.2016

Tanya's Diary

The nurse at the counter slipped me a note. 'Are you having suicidal thoughts?'

"Yes," I nodded.

"We're keeping you overnight", she said. "It's nice up there, I think you'll like it."

You will see a lot of movies in your life. Sometimes the movies have exaggerated situations to make it more exciting to watch. I found out that a Psychiatric Ward is a real thing. You really do write with crayons because anything else could be used as a weapon. There are no toilet seats. No mirrors. That one I was cool with. You return your soap and toothpaste when you're done with it in the allotted time. You eat supervised and your tray is reviewed after you're finished to make sure you didn't steal the plastic knife. You have group therapy sessions, make crafts, and talk with other people with problems far worse than your own. You're scared.

But for me… I was happy. Because there were no children. No whining. No screaming in my face, or throwing of food, or four hundred messes to clean up. No snack snack Snack SNACKS! No potty accidents everywhere all the time on everything! No one calling me Mama!

9

4.7.2014

Baby Journal

Pregnancy stick was positive. I'd never taken one of those before! I left it on the sink in the bathroom for Jason to find when he got home from work. When I knew he'd gone into the bathroom, I waited outside the door.

He opened the door back up and asked, "What's your little stick thing mean?"

"Means there's a baby in there", I said.

"Well that's cool", he said "I didn't know if we could do that or not. Are you okay?"

I told him I felt good and was nervous. He hugged me and my eyes filled with tears.

4.7.2014

Tanya's Diary

OH GOD... I knew it. It's like when I didn't study for my Life Insurance exam way back when and after I finished, the screen popped up with a big 'You failed' and I was like... yep, I deserved that. But then I had to go back to the office and explain to my boss (my Mom) that I am a failure and she wasted money on my schooling for this and now I have to face the consequences. Same.

But what are the consequences here? I have a baby. I've never babysat a baby before. I've never changed a diaper. Wait, yes I have. My nephew once filled his diaper up so badly that it was traveling south into his socks, so I had to take action. I remember vomiting. I also remember not wanting children.

Not for a long time anyway. Okay. I'm okay. We've been married six years. Neither of us knows anything about babies. They eat, cry, and sleep, yeah? That's essentially what I do. We gotta procreate some time. So everybody says. We get a lot of guff for not having any kids yet. Nearly every day someone says, "So...when are you having children?" I started saying, "We're not sure if we can". It turns some heads. I don't ask you when you're going to go die; leave me alone. What if I were trying to have kids and struggling? Then you'd have that visual.

I feel sick.

13

5.23.2014

Baby Journal

Told our families about the coming babe. Very exciting. Mom cried.

5.23.2014

Tanya's Diary

We've got this marriage thing down, we may as well take the next step and make more people that look like us. I hope they don't look like me. Come on recessive genes!

Jason is so good looking. As soon as I saw him I was like 'Earth needs more of THAT!' Thus, the procreating. He's also nice.

Seriously though, isn't that why people have children? At least a little bit? To see what they look like? I wonder if people ever give them back. "Dang it, got your Mom's red hair on this one, let's try again, this time gimme some blue eye genes and I'll give some blonde hair genes. Operation procreation, take two." That seems a little insensitive.

I'm going to get FAAAAAAAAAAAAAAAATTTTTTT!

I'm a nervous pooper. I'll never poop again! If there's always a kid around, how am I supposed to poop in peace? Poop a piece of poop in peace. Poop.

Daycare! Right. That's right. You get to put your kid in daycare. That's when I'll poop. So I guess I'll just keep doing my nine to five insurance agent from home job and take care of the baby at the same time. Fortunately, with Mom as my boss, she will allow that. She has allowed me to be a work at home wife with all these military moves we have made so far. I have the best job, the best boss, and I always look forward to my work. I know I can do this.

15

6.23.2014

Baby Journal

You make me puke whenever I brush my teeth. I love you still. I am just over fifteen weeks and beginning to show a belly. I weigh one hundred fifteen pounds. Your Dad takes me to the gym every week for 'Zumba' and he works out too. We love fitness. I love to run. I hope you do too! We are getting more and more excited to meet you. I'm told you are the size of an orange now.

6.23.2014

Tanya's Diary

NOOOOOOOOOOOOO!!!!! I heard horror stories about how the smell or taste of such and such made people so sick while they were pregnant. Coffee! My one true love! Why must you betray me! I keep drinking you every morning, but you smell so terrible.

Please God don't let me get any stretch marks. And no C-Section scar either! THANK YOU!

So far nobody can tell I'm pregnant. I do like that. Makes me feel skinny, which is really all I've got going for me. I'm not nice. I'm not fashionable or smart. I can't cook. I don't have nice hair or skin or any sort of feminine attribute really. I don't caress the world with my cute world views (I don't even have world views, if I did it would be ... spherical). I don't make lotions or soaps or hemp (what's hemp?). I can't sing or dance. When I do, people laugh like they thought I was trying to make them laugh. I'm like, "... Right? Yeah, that was silly ... what I did there. I'd never actually dance like that. You're welcome... for the laugh. I did it for you."

I slow dance pretty well though. So I've been told. By no one. I think about what it'd be like to be told I'm good at it though. That's something.

7.22.2014

Baby Journal

Today we find out your gender. This is the first time we will see you on the screen I am told. I am so excited. I am twenty-one weeks along now and I have not yet felt you move in there! I weigh one hundred seventeen pounds. So nervous… But God is in control and we already love you so much. Olive Garden to celebrate you tonight. We would go to Red Lobster (my favorite), but I'm not allowed to have seafood yet.

YOU'RE A BOY!

The ultrasound technician says you are perfectly healthy. Can I tell you a secret? When your Dad and I prayed, we asked that you would be a perfectly healthy boy! Praise Jesus! We wanted you, our first child, to be a boy because we feel it is important for any child after you to have a big brother to love and protect them, and be the good influence they can look up to when we aren't available. This might be the best day of my life!

7.22.2014

Tanya's Diary

Jason keeps telling me I can't have seafood and asking me if I've taken my vitamins and have I made sure not to work out too hard or lift anything over the weight of a plate? I held a sneeze in 3 hours ago, is that okay honey? I also peed 33 times in the past 33 minutes. My back hurts so bad I could cry all day long. I can only sleep on my back and even then, I'm in agony. Hope I'm not drinking too much caffeine for your baby! Iced tea really stinks to drink in the morning just so you know. Just what I want to wake me up, an iced cold glass of NOTHING! Nothing is good COLD in the morning! Coffee, I don't even remember your flavor. You failure of a beverage. I hate you. Oh, I miss you. Come back to me.

I really wish there were an option for the married couple to choose who gets to carry the baby for the pregnancy. I know we would have chosen Jason. He could eat Chinese buffet for breakfast, lunch, and dinner, and still lose weight. Piece of work. I'd stand behind him in line and yell "You can't have that!" Haha. That's fun. Made myself laugh.

I crave curly fries, candy, and pickles. But who doesn't?

I'm so tired.

Why are these prenatal vitamins the size of a mobile home? Who eats mobile homes? I could cut this thing up into 12 pieces, feed the 5,000 and have 7 baskets of fish left over. Excitingly, if I swallow the thing before noon, I throw it up and get to do it again after noon.

8.1.2014

Baby Journal

Today we went to the store and registered for all sorts of things we would like to have to fill your bedroom and to take care of you!

8.1.2014

Tanya's Diary

Nursery. Excuse me, woman at the store. Apparently, babies have a special name for the room their bed is in. My room, with my bed in it, is called my bedroom.

We registered for our baby shower and learned that there is a whole baby vocabulary we've been missing out on. Like... swaddle, onesie, bassinet, carrier, breast pump, nipple shield, teethers, boppies and bumbos. Do we really need all these things? Can't we just get diapers and wipes and give you baths in the sink? I love you, like... a lot. But I don't even know how to use any of these gadgets or why you'd need to. There was a bottle warmer at the store. Isn't that what microwaves are for? Milk tastes better cold, just a heads up.

It was actually one of the best dates I've ever had with Jason though. Seeing his eyes light up with sheer excitement and confusion the same way mine did was great. We were both mostly concerned with the jogging stroller. He is going to be a great Daddy. When it came to the car seat aisle, I was like, "I like the yellow one". He was fidgeting with them making sure they're super safe and that he understood how to get them in and out of the car. My plan is to avoid the knowledge part so as to get out of having to do much. I'll just throw out the owner's manual when we get it.

8.25.2014

Baby Journal

You are moving around in there nowadays! I can hardly focus on anything else once I feel you kick or squirm. Your Dad lights up whenever he feels you too. For a while, you would move and I would tell him, so he was excited to feel my belly, and then you were quiet. I think you love your Dad's touch. He's a great guy. I hope you look up to him. He will always protect us.

We had a baby shower thrown for us last week by my friends Sarah, Megan, and your Grandma Paige. We received so many gifts for you! I can hardly wait to set up your room. We love you baby. So excited to meet you!

8.25.2014

Tanya's Diary

It is so hard to get anything done with you scraping my belly button all day long. It is the creepiest, weirdest feeling ever.

And why does everyone want to know if I'm breastfeeding? I think they know something I don't. I'm glad to live so far away from family for this time in our lives, so I can figure it out on my own and call for help when I need it instead of having to hear opinions I don't want.

My favorite right now is, "Oh Tanya, you need a baby swing. You HAVE to have a baby swing." Don't tell me what I have to have. My baby will go to sleep when I tell it to go to sleep. When can babies understand what you say? I don't know what I'm doing. I wonder if anybody got us a baby swing. Oh good. Dodged a bullet. Also, fourteen booger suckers. What does everyone know that I don't know!? Why did people get us so many blankets? I can't wait for someone else to get pregnant so I can give them all this extra crap.

It's weird going through all this stuff that's not mine to set up a room that's completely not for me. Call me selfish, but I could really have used like one gift with a bag of chips in it. Just one. A small bag even, like the one you got in your meal deal at Subway last week. Any sort of evidence that I matter in all this.

23

9.9.2014

Baby Journal

Your room is finished. This might sound odd, but I'm not afraid of anything yet. We have less than three months until you show your face to the world, and we are so ready.

My back hurts very badly every day but it's not your fault. I love you. I am ready to be a Mom, your Mom. We have had your named picked out for quite some time. You are named after the most wonderful angel mentioned in the Bible. We haven't shared your name with anyone because we want it to be a surprise! I went through baby pictures of me the other day. I was kind of chubby! But I was happy. We want you to be so happy too! You will have hard times on this earth, but God will get you through them. He promises us this. I have had many hard times myself but I made it through them all! And now, our lives seem so complete to know you are coming soon. I am trying to eat very healthy for you, so eat up! You are fifteen inches long and weigh two and a half pounds these days!

9.9.2014

Tanya's Diary

Yes, I'm pregnant. Quit looking at me everyone. No, I didn't get fat off the pizza. You're safe to eat the pizza. Well maybe not, but quit looking at me! I don't look at you! I have never looked at a pregnant woman before in my life the way people are looking at me. It's like I'm a parade float. Don't mind me, just came out into public for everyone to oogle at my misshapen body and inability to sit down in the normal allotted time. Yes, I'm going to eat all this. And you know what! I always ate this much! Quit making fun of me!

The worst was at the sub place. I ordered a meatball sub the way I like it, with lettuce, tomato, black olives, and mayo. They laughed at me and said, "Must be a pregnancy craving, look what she just had me put on this sub." I could have cried. I think my emotions are weird right now. They're right, no normal human being would eat that, just me. I should have ordered a turkey and cheese like the rest of the world. And been sad. Like I am. I wouldn't make fun of you if you ordered an olive loaf sub with pizza and boogers on top, just so you know. I'd be like... my boogers or yours? Or Jim's? He's got big ones. Here's a free brownie. I made it with my feet.

10.20.2014

Baby Journal

[no entry]

10.20.2014

Tanya's Diary

I love seeing my husband interact with people. I love him. It is one of the most honorable things, being his wife. I am the one you just don't know how to predict, and he is the noble knight, the same guy when he wakes up til he lays down. How does he do that? Together, we're hip. But once I'm without him, I'm like a wave tossed by the sea. I can't hold my head up for long. I'm sad.

When he went off to 'boot camp' years ago, I learned a lot about myself. I learned that I no longer know who I am without my husband. My favorite color is yellow, I think. I like Jesus, chips, fitness, and clean comedy. I know these things.

11.10.2014

Baby Journal

Your due date is December 5TH. You should be here in less than a month. Your Dad and I are realizing how quiet our lives are and we are so excited for you to fill that spot! We have everything as ready as possible. My body has gone through a lot up until now and I am very tired. The doctor has given me a few pills to take to make sure you and I are both healthy. I look forward to the pills every day because I know they help you, otherwise pills are gross!

When you show your face here soon, we get to take time off from work to take care of you. It is almost Thanksgiving, and Grandma Paige and Grandpa Ron might be able to come see you when you are born! They live all the way up in Michigan. We live one thousand miles away, in North Carolina. If they make it here, that is a wonderful gift!

I weigh about one hundred forty pounds now and you weigh about six pounds! Once I am healthy again after having you, I look forward to taking you outside in the jogging stroller. It has been about six months since I last went for a run and I miss it very much! We will have a lot of fun together.

11.10.2014

Tanya's Diary

I feel swear words toward these pills. This paper isn't big enough for the swear words I feel for these pills. This paper isn't big enough to hold the pills. I'd rather eat this sheet of paper than have to swallow all these stupid pills. I have negative feelings toward the pills.

I think I gain a pound a day now. I'm so fat. I can't even sit down. I lay down and I can hardly breath. The baby is like... in my ribs and pressing down on my ... everything! I'm walking along (scooting) last night with Jason and the baby kicked me in my crotch. What's that about?! Took my breath away like falling on the bar on the boy bike. Only internal.

I'm pretty sure I see a stretch mark forming on my belly button.

GET OUT!

I can't believe Mom and Dad are trying to visit for the coming babe. I am so blessed by just the thought. I love to show my Mom what I've done. She always knows what I need, whether it be a hug, a card, a just because gift, or words. I want to be that kind of Mom. And Dad, well, I witnessed a robbery once and I called him right after. I was sobbing so hard he couldn't understand me. I don't know why I called him. I got in a car accident once and was struggling so badly to breath I thought I would die in seconds. I called him. I needed to know who sang that song right then, so I called him. We were locked out of our house and knew we had to break a window but which one? So I called him. The cool thing about my Dad is... he always answers.

11.25.2014

Baby Journal

[no entry]

11.25.2014

Tanya's Diary

Get out. I hurt.

Get out! I hurt all over.

GET OUT!

12.1.2014

Baby Journal

Gabriel. That is your name.

Happy Birthday My Son! Today you entered the world. Eight pounds nine ounces and twenty-one and a half inches long. You are healthy. You have a full head of crazy brown hair. You are incredible. I love to watch you sleep, you are so cute. Your Dad loves you so much too! He is holding you as I write this.

And guess what … I got a special meal today as a congratulation from the hospital. Lobster!

12.1.2014

Tanya's Diary

I don't understand how I'm alive.

I was induced because for whatever reason, I was having increasingly painful contractions but not dilating (gross), and then Gabriel's heart was showing distress.

After 14 hours of ow, I had to have a stupid c-section. Mark my stomach off the list of good things I had going for me...now I've just got the bottoms of my feet - which are so swollen right now that Jason squeezes them and his handprint stays. I can't walk. I feel like I was cut in half and sewn back together. I'm afraid to look. They told me I have to get up and go to the bathroom today. I still can't feel my feet so I don't know if it'll happen. A lady came in and wiped my body from armpit to thigh. That was exciting. I feel like Gilbert Grape's Mom.

I farted in front of my nurse. A big one. I was under some contraction inducing medicine and an epidural also later on and had no control over anything and WHAM! Pretty sure we had Mexican food the night before because it smelled like nachos. Rotten nachos. It was the first time I recall ever saying the words, "was that me?"

I could have gone without that.

Jason took such good care of me. I can't believe he's mine. Gabriel doesn't look anything like either of us. His hair is dark. The doctor showed him to me and I was like 'okay'. Where's the blonde hair and blue eyes? They told me it comes later. Must be a rebate thing.

33

12.4.2014

Baby Journal

Today we brought you home.

We washed your greasy hair and your lips made a cute little O shape. You are so fragile and sweet.

We are so excited to have you here with us, we will all sleep together in the living room tonight.

12.4.2014

Tanya's Diary

The doctors gave us a few instructions (why weren't there MORE INSTRUCTIONS?!) on how to take care of the babe and what to look for. The big things were a sunken head and diarrhea. "Bring him back immediately", they said, "if he has diarrhea."

"Okay", we said with huge eyes.

As Jason was changing Gabriel's diaper, he noticed ALL of his poop looks like diarrhea. He's right. If that came outta me, that's diarrhea. All day long.

He just called the nurse and we're headed to the E.R.

Why did they let us take him home? We don't know what we're doing.

Evening note added: Apparently baby poop looks like diarrhea. So we've decided to cross out the concern for diarrhea because we'll never know if you have it. And we learned that we are 'those' parents. But it was really wonderful to hear the doctor say that you appear totally healthy. Worth it.

12.15.2014

Baby Journal

It has been two very busy weeks with you joining our family! We have agreed that this has been the best vacation imaginable! You are the most beautiful thing we've ever seen and we look forward to every waking Moment with you! So what have I missed...

Grandma Paige and Grandpa Ron did come all the way here from Michigan. They stayed at our home while your Dad and I had to stay in the hospital four days. They came to the hospital to hold you and bring us goodies each day. Grandpa Ron kept making me laugh; he's silly. I kept telling him to stop making me laugh because my belly hurt SO BAD, but he can't help it. We had to watch the news on the TV at the hospital instead of something funny because oh I hurt. They left back to Michigan after giving us meals and love.

At one point in the hospital, you were taken away from us to have a procedure done, and we realized how much we love you. We were so afraid to lose you after all we'd been through to bring you into the world!

Our drive home from the hospital, you cried the entire time. You suddenly stopped crying and your Daddy and I looked at each other in fear, pulled the car over and learned you'd just fallen asleep. We checked to make sure you were breathing. Wow. That was so scary.

I love you Gabriel. Oh I love you.

12.15.2014

Tanya's Diary

My NIPPLES! It's like the chappiest of chapped lips being dipped in salt water at all times. And then you're like, 'just kidding, let's suck on those again!' How am I not bleeding?

As soon as we got out of the hospital, my body started to have curiosity toward coffee again. That. Is. So. Weird. So we went to the coffee shop drive thru. (I always thought the drive thru was for people who were too lazy to get out of the car and walk inside. Turns out it's also for people who have forgotten what sleep is, have been cut in half and can't walk, and have a child they spent an hour buckling into a seat contraption and now have no clue how to get out.) Anyway, ordered my first cup of coffee post baby, Jason handed it to me, and I fell asleep holding it in the air. Never took a sip. Something about just having it gave me comfort that everything would be all right.

I'm never going anywhere without Jason. How do single Moms do things with babies? You poor things. Seriously. He gets up for a bathroom break and I'm like, "don't go!"

I don't think tomorrow will come. I've seen every minute of every day for the past 15 days. There is no break from this. This is forever. Jason thinks he's doing me a favor, offering to hold him while I go take a shower. So I get up and Gabriel wakes up and wants to eat. And puke on me again. And milk is shooting out of my nipples across the room. I could totally win at that clown water game at the carnival right now.

12.21.2014

Baby Journal

We brought you to church with us today for the first time!

Unfortunately, we didn't make it inside the building. We made the drive, put the car in park and you puked all over yourself, your seat and the car.

We'll try again next week. I am excited to hold you and dance to the music together.

12.21.2014

Tanya's Diary

So apparently the diaper bag is for every time you go out of the house, not just for sleepovers. We registered for one, but I didn't know you're supposed to take it with you every time you go out? It would have come in handy today. With the puke. Everywhere. My poor little Honda Civic. I hate everyone with a van right now.

It's sort of okay we didn't get to go to church. We were late anyway. Minutes into the drive, we looked in the backseat and realized we'd forgotten the huge, obnoxious, turquoise booger sucker. The nurse said, "keep this in the car seat at all times". Jason and I decided if we didn't turn around to go find the booger sucker, we'd be the worst parents in the world and you'd surely die. So, we turned around and got it from home.

That was stupid. I want to be a good Mom, but seriously? Can a booger get so big that a baby will die? Why MUST this thing be in the car seat at all times? They didn't show us a video on that. Just the 'don't shake your baby' video. That was a good one. I hope I get to watch that more often.

1.15.2015

Baby Journal

Hi Gabriel. You are just over a month and a half now. You are so fun! For a time, you would wake us up every two hours to feed you and change your diaper. Nowadays you are lasting three or four hours and sometimes you let us sleep a good five hours at night. We appreciate that. I believe you have colic, which makes you cry anytime you are awake. It hurts our hearts to see you in such distress, but we are doing everything we can for you. I no longer am eating dairy because I've heard that could be hurting your tummy.

I work from home and you hang with me all day. You really like your swing. I try to play with you and show you your toys but you just cry. Cry cry cry. So, you swing a lot.

1.15.2015

Tanya's Diary

I have no idea what I'm doing. I just want to hold you like I see other Moms do. Other Moms love their babies and they snuggle into their necks and give hugs and kisses. You just scream into my ears and I put you in the swing because I have no idea what to do. Everyone says, "At this age, you just give him what he wants." I DON'T KNOW WHAT YOU WANT! I've tried everything!

I had a nurse come to the house and she and I did everything with you that babies do... eat, play, snuggle, walk around with you, take you for a stroller ride. You cry every waking minute of every day. She verified that you are a colicky baby. She says it just 'is what it is'.

I will not shake my baby.

I will not shake my baby.

Jason and I were chatting today in bed (because we can't talk while the baby is awake since he's literally crying all the time) about Abraham and how he was called to sacrifice his son Isaac. Jason was all, "I can't imagine ever sacrificing Gabe. That must have been so awful."

I wonder if Abraham was a work from home Dad and Isaac was colicky. I'm so tired.

I don't know what I'd do without this baby swing. Maybe Abraham didn't have a swing. Oooohh, that's it. Nah, Isaac was much older then. Maybe he broke a window. And lied about it. Sinner.

41

1.19.2015

Baby Journal

You smiled today! Finally!

You smile when I visit you each morning. It is wonderful. And you reeeeallly like

your pacifier. I'm cool with that.

1.19.2015

Tanya's Diary

We took you out this evening, just to the store and home. Wouldn't you know it. My first day where I felt like you might actually be enjoying life because this pacifier has calmed you during your waking Moments... some older Mom comes up to me and says, "oh honey, you don't want him to have that pacifier, his teeth will grow in crooked and you'll never be able to take it away from him."

Why.

Do I have a sign on me that says 'Please give me negative feedback about how I'm doing'?

I'd really like to take that sign off.

I am told all day long that what I'm doing isn't good enough. From 5am to 8pm, I am a human punching bag. If not from Gabriel, from my coworkers. The only time my coworkers talk to me is to tell me I did something wrong. Then Jason comes home and I can't help but feel ashamed the house is a mess, there is no dinner ready, and I look and smell like vomit. Or rotten milk. It's the same right now.

Let me know if I get something right. Anybody.

43

2.1.2015

Baby Journal

Gabriel, today you are 2 months old! Wow! I had to put away all of your 'newborn' size clothes because you are too big for them! Big boy! You have completed my life Gabriel. Without you on earth, I was very happy, but I was missing something and it was you. We take very good care of you Gabriel. Mom and Dad love you so much!

You are about to make sounds, I can tell! Every day I talk with you about monkeys and lions. I can hardly wait to hear your voice and watch you crawl!

When you lay on your tummy, you can roll over onto your back.

You take a bath each night and your Dad scrubs you clean. You watch him very closely to make sure he's doing a good job.

You still cry a lot, but I try not to take it personal.

You are very handsome! Everyone says so! I have given you two haircuts already! Your hair stands straight up in the center and you look very cool.

Your Great Grandma Dotti died today. She was very old and weak. We are happy to know that she is in heaven now. She was very excited for you to be born. I remember she said "I can go now" after she got to meet you. You are very special to her. Her first great grandchild!

44

2.1.2015

Tanya's Diary

Sometimes I wonder if you just roll because you hate 'tummy time' so much, or if you actually have acquired this new skill. You scream the Moment I bend down to set you down. It's like you know I'm going to put you down. But you cry if I hold you too! Work with me would ya! If I didn't know any better, I'd say you're allergic to the carpet or something. Maybe you think I like your screamo singing voice. I do not.

Whenever I try to give you a bath, I can feel Jason looking at me. His body language tells me I'm doing it wrong. It's not the best feeling, but I'm with you all day, if he wants this task, I'm more than happy to lighten the load. I wish he helped because he wanted to help though instead of because I'm doing it wrong. Maybe he is, I don't know. I don't know what I'm doing. I'm trying so hard I could cry.

When you get older, if you have this same haircut, you may not make friends too quickly.

2.26.2015

Baby Journal

Oh Gabriel, I love you so much! You are growing so fast and you are coming to know who we are. You light up whenever you see our faces. You say "ooh" now, just like a monkey! You 'talk' with me and smile so much. I tickle you and you smile and screech!

We took you on your first ride in an airplane! You didn't mind it, you actually fell asleep. Okay, you cried the whole time, and fell asleep crying. The air pressure is so noisy on an airplane though that I don't think we made any enemies. Everyone on the plane said you were so cute and they told us we did a good job parenting you.

2.26.2015

Tanya's Diary

'Good Job'.

Thank you.

I can still see the man flashing a thumbs up sign over to me from across the

aisle.

3.4.2015

Baby Journal

You giggled for the first time!

3.4.2015

Tanya's Diary

My coffee cup is always too far away. It doesn't matter where I put it. I sit down to nurse you and I can't reach it.

It's okay. I'll just microwave it for the ninth time and forget about it until I go to microwave something else and knock it over. It'll spill all down the microwave, onto the stove and onto the floor. Then I'll clean it up. Because that's what I do.

49

3.12.2015

Baby Journal

Gabriel, you are a smart boy. And so tall! Maybe you will be taller than Dad!

3.12.2015

Tanya's Diary

I type about 105 wpm. With you in my office, I type 2 letters, let's say A and B, you cry, I roll you over back onto your tummy, I type 2 more letters, you cry, I roll you back onto your tummy, and repeat. I can't do this.

I wake up at 3am just so I can get any work done.

The office calls me throughout the day, to tell me when I've done something wrong, and I can't hear the phone ring over your crying. It's right next to me.

I cry every day. I haven't stopped crying since you were born. How am I supposed to do this? I need my job. I want my job. I want to understand you.

How do you put a baby down for a nap? I don't get it. I read the internet and it says, "then put your baby down for a 30 minute to 2 hour nap". What does it mean to 'put your baby down for a nap'? I need a video. Preferably one with the mother crying in the other room so I can feel like I'm not alone. I lay Gabe down in his crib and he cries for 45 minutes until I finally give up and put him in the swing. He falls asleep in that thing after 10 minutes of crying. Is that bad parenting, putting him in the swing all the time? I want some help. I need a break. I don't know anyone here. My neighbor came out and introduced herself to me the other day but she works all day so it's not like I can use her help to watch Gabe while I work for a few minutes.

3.15.2015

Baby Journal

Dad is on a field expedition for 10 days so it's been just you and me. We went to church today and you did great. You bounced on my legs and we sang and danced. We sang 'How He loves us' by David Crowder Band and it was wonderful. I clipped your nails today. Dad usually does this while I hold you, but since he isn't here, I had to try on my own. I clipped two of your nails too short and you are bleeding. I'm sorry Gabe. You are very tough and did not cry much. I rinsed your hand under running water, kissed it, and put band-aids on your fingers. I am very glad your Dad will come home soon so we can all be a team again.

3.15.2015

Tanya's Diary

Now I really am alone.

I don't know what I'm doing.

My heart is in my throat at all times. I'm so scared.

I can't sleep. Every noise is someone trying to get me. And now I have

your life to protect too. I wish I knew someone here so I could feel like anyone

would know I were missing if we were taken. But I don't. And they won't. I don't

matter. I'm that person on the news that you skim past because you're like, "Oh that

is so sad, don't know her". Next. Free ice cream cones at Dairy Queen? Sign me

up!

3.16.2015

Baby Journal

[no entry]

3.16.2015

Tanya's Diary

I survived the night.

This is how it's been for so long. I've followed Jason from school to school for his military moves, working from wherever I've lived. I've lived alone in all these places because he has to live in the barracks during school, even though we've been married so long prior to joining the military. I've been terrified every Moment, day and night. My first day of my first move out to be near him, I moved all my things into my new place and waited outside for him, to see him for the first time in months. A man darted at me and chased me. I ducked into my apartment before he saw which one I'd gone into. That doesn't help my thoughts.

When the frogs quit croaking, I wonder why and I jump up to peak out the window, my shotgun in hand. The neighbor's dog barks. Why? Is someone in my yard? I jump up, my shotgun in hand. I see a shadow go by my window, I jump up with my shotgun in my hand. The worst was when the power went out after I'd just moved into my Texas apartment. I was sure someone was going to come get me, sure they'd cut my power. Then a group of vehicles circled around my apartment building with their music blaring. I was sure that was so my screams wouldn't be heard. I didn't sleep. I called the police. "Maybe you shouldn't live alone", they said. "You're right", I said. But Jason is finally done with schooling and we are together again. We've made it this far. He'll be back in just 9 days. 9 days. I can do this.

3.25.2015

Baby Journal

You are so much fun my Gabriel. We tickle your armpits and you giggle.
You love to see your face in the mirror. You are very handsome. And strong! You
hold your head up very well now and you love to sit up and stand on Dad's chest!
You dropped your ball today and thought that was so funny! We love you Gabriel.

3.25.2015

Tanya's Diary

I'll do anything to hear you giggle.

4.7.2015

Baby Journal

Hi Gabe. You are four months old now! You roll over a lot, even in your sleep. Sometimes you get stuck in the wrong position and cry for us to come help. You are currently sick for the first time. You have a fever, sore throat, cough, and snotty nose. We watched a long movie with you last night called Interstellar. You don't usually sit still long enough for us to watch movies so this was really cool. You like TV.

We took you golfing once so far. You slept in your stroller most of the time. I love you buddy.

-   Mom

4.7.2015

Tanya's Diary

I am so sick today. I puked while changing your diaper and went right back to it. We picked a good spot for the garbage bin. An inch to the right and it would have been stain city all over that carpet, wall, trim, self.

I then had diarrhea. I put you in the crib and let you scream while I lost a few pounds. My head hurts and I'm so dizzy I can hardly take steps. I think it's a stomach bug because I heard that's going around. No break for Moms. I saw a commercial once that said parents don't get a sick day. I can't believe how true it is. I couldn't call in sick if I wanted to, I'd still have to nurse you. This is the hardest job in the world. I just want to sleep.

4.8.2015

Baby Journal

[no entry]

4.8.2015

Tanya's Diary

I am irate.

Had to call my buddy Megan to calm me down I am so angry I could slam every door and throw every dish in this house!

Jason is sick now. His turn. Guess who got to call in sick!

My first thought was, "Yay, now he'll see what I went through and he'll help me take care of Gabe so I can get some work done. After he slept for 12 hours straight, I realized I married the wrong man.

After he slept 10 hours more, I realized this whole Mom job is just crap. CRAP! You get yelled at, pooped on, puked on all day long, and NO PAY. Nothing! I want to be the Dad. Come on! Seriously.

Jason and I ran into one of his co-workers the other day at the grocery store and he asked what I do and I mentioned I stay with Gabe all day while I work and he said something along the lines of, "Oh that must be so rewarding, being a parent". I said, "No, it's not. I love my son, but parenting isn't for everyone. I'm pretty sure it's not for me but I'm too far into the maze, I can't find my way out!" Then he laughed and I was like… I don't know why he's laughing. I said it pretty sincere. My eye was twitching and everything.

4.11.2015

Baby Journal

Today I carried you around and you watched me chop up onions, celery, potatoes, eggs, whew! It took all day to make my very first potato salad but it turned out tasty! You fell asleep watching golf with us today, The Masters Championship. We are rooting for Jordan Spieth.

4.11.2015

Tanya's Diary

I wish I could fall asleep watching golf. If I tried to fall asleep, Jason would be like, "Did you see that?!" Then I'd have to pretend I wasn't asleep and be all, "Right? That shot... that he just hit...it was so good. Like I don't even know how he did that, he must have a new trainer. Or maybe it's the shoes. We should get some of those shoes for you, I just love you so much. And I know how important golf is to you. That's why I was watching it."

4.17.2015

Baby Journal

      Gabriel, you are getting so big! You fell asleep in your crib all by yourself last night. You giggle every day for us. You like drumming. Can't wait to take you out golfing this weekend!

4.17.2015

Tanya's Diary

My first sip of coffee is like an intimate kiss. I move in real close and take a sip while it's still resting on the counter. Too full to pick up. Why can I not overfill my cup? Is it even a problem? I think I'm mad about it. I really just like the French vanilla creamer. I could write poems about it. I won't though because that'd be weird. And no one would read them. They'd think about it and then they'd be like, "I could be doing anything else right now". And then they'd go do something else.

5.1.2015

Baby Journal

Hi Gabe, guess what!? Today you are five months old, wow! Life with you has gotten more and more fun. Grandma Paige came to stay with us this week and we have had a great time! We went to Emerald Isle and took you to coffee shops, thrift stores, and have gone on lots of walks! We love to go outside. You like the grass. You are so rambunctious. You move all over the place on the floor. You do push-ups and are very eager to crawl. You say 'goo'. It makes my heart skip a beat every time.

You dove head first into the water filled bathtub the other day and freaked me right out! But you weren't scared. I picked you up out of the water so quickly, like a lifeguard!

You love Grandma Paige. You smile and giggle with her. She is very fun and loves you so much! She wants to take you camping some day!

5.1.2015

Tanya's Diary

Five months old. I alerted the family that you are 5 months old and they were all, "Oh it goes by so fast, doesn't it?!!!"

No! Not at all.

I've seen every minute of these past five months. I know exactly what time the sun comes up and goes down and where it will shine into what window and how warm and there is a lizard caught in between the screen and window in my office and he looks at me all day long. I tell him all about my day. He is turning purple. He might need help.

I hate camping. There are certain life luxuries that I think I now deserve. Now that I'm a Mom, I'll take any hand out I can get. Like a shower, a bed, chips, and electricity. Someone invented them, I thank them, I earn them, I keep them. I do not backtrack and sleep in the woods for bugs to eat me.

I love my Mom. She just knows I need help and flew all the way down here from Michigan to be with me and help me a few days. She loves Gabe. She is amazing. She told me I'm a good Mom. She said it out loud.

5.10.2015

Baby Journal

      It is Mother's Day.

      Your Daddy dreamt up this day and took us all out for coffee and for a walk. Just what I like to do. It was very sweet of him.

5.10.2015

Tanya's Diary

Why do I even leave the house? So I can go be a Mom someplace else? I have to pump milk and pack up a duffle bag of diapers, wipes, burp cloths, bottles, extra clothes, pacifiers, and booger suckers just to leave the house and for what? So I can do what I'm already doing at home, just in another location, where people are looking at me when you cry and thinking 'Oh wow, they shouldn't have left the house'.

All I want is a babysitter.

For the next 16 years.

5.14.2015

Baby Journal

Gabriel, you are so funny and strong! You roll around and push your whole body up now! You make a bridge! Whenever Dad or I go into your room to get you out of bed, you are wide awake looking at us, in that bridge! So silly! You giggle and screech and play with your voice. I like your screech the best and I think you know it because you look at me and do it even if we aren't doing anything.

You eat oatmeal now. You are a good eater. Some babies struggle and make big messes. I pray you stay so good. You are our daily blessing. I love you Gabe. Oops I almost forgot, you also sit up on your own!

You go to the nursery at church now every Sunday to hang out with other kids your age! So cool!

You are so handsome and funny that we have a hard time looking away from you.

70

5.14.2015

Tanya's Diary

Wow. I held Jason's hand at church this Sunday. Because we put Gabe in the nursery for the first time. I actually teared up when we let him go. My first time apart from him. When service was over, Jason and I were both walking so quickly to go pick him up. As other parents were walking in our direction, holding their children they'd picked up, we glanced at every single kid to make sure no one stole our kid. I've got a lot invested in this one.

He cried the entire time, they said. They gave him his bottle, and once it was finished, he cried the rest of the time. As sad as it is, it was cool to hear he's not just crying around us. He actually just hates life in general.

5.20.2015

Baby Journal

You do the 'worm' and travel all over the floors now! Oh dear… and you blow raspberries! And you have two bottom teeth coming in! And you drool everywhere! I walk you around and you suck on my shoulder and the drool runs down my arm, then my leg.

Gabriel buddy I love you.

5.20.2015

Tanya's Diary

Took you for a walk tonight and a girl in her early twenties stopped to chat with me. She shared with me that she just found out she is pregnant and said, "Wow you look so great for just having a baby. That's total motivation for me. If I look as good as you after I have my baby, I'll be so happy!"

I think she was trying to give me a compliment, but I said, "I don't have time to feed myself. This is just my body wasting away."

I don't know why she laughed. I was pretty sincere.

Jason said I wasn't very encouraging and need to find what adults call a 'filter'.

I tell him if I didn't say what I wanted, nobody would laugh and the world would be a boring place. So I give them something to laugh at.

He tried to say something else but I interrupted with a "you're welcome".

He didn't laugh. He doesn't laugh at my jokes. He's like my own personal Eeyore. So fun to have around. At least he's not that gopher with the screechy lisp. I'd be busy that day.

5.22.2015

Baby Journal

You laughed so hard at us shaking a box of cereal today. Made us so happy.

5.22.2015

Tanya's Diary

[no entry]

5.30.2015

Baby Journal

Your Grandma Diane and Aunt Nicole came down from Michigan last week. We took you to the beach! You think the sand is cool but you weren't quite ready for the water. It is a bit loud and windy at the beach too, so maybe that bothered you. I am very excited to make a big sand castle with you someday Gabriel.

Buddy boy, you were mad at me the other day because I turned my head away from you as I was brushing my teeth. I had to spit out my toothpaste. You were on Mom and Dad's bed and you cried and crawled across the bed and fell onto the floor. I was terrified you might have been hurt but you are just fine. Oh Gabriel. You've got to be patient. You had me so scared. I love you buddy, be careful so we can all keep playing together! God kept all your body parts intact this time!

5.30.2015

Tanya's Diary

I am a terrible Mom. How could I have let you fall off the bed? If someone finds out, will they take him away? I don't know the rules. A Mom's gotta brush her teeth though right?

I looked up a few things I do, like brushing my teeth, putting Gabe in the car seat in a shopping cart, leaving you in the car for a millisecond so I can go drop a letter in the letterbox at the post office and then come right back.... Am I actually a bad Mom? All of these things are frowned upon, but what am I supposed to do? How do they expect a Mom to do anything? Am I supposed to let you hang off my nipples and walk around like a cat with her kitten stuck to her? Poor cats. I remember seeing kitten Mommies and their eyes just roll in the back of their head like they're so ticked off while their kittens are nursing. It's true. It is so degrading having someone suck on you. Like, where do you look? What do you do during that time? Not only am I being sucked on, I'm being kicked and punched and slapped. Then puked on, so I can do it all again to refill your now empty belly.

This is the worst job in the world.

6.2.2015

Baby Journal

You are six months old now my Gabriel. And guess what? You crawl! I can
hardly turn away for a Moment and you're already following me into the kitchen or
down the hallway. Silly boy. You pick yourself up and climb up me.

-   Mom

Evening note added: You bashed your mouth on your Dad's metal canteen
tonight. You have a bloody mouth but no scars! Oh baby boy, I love your face, be
careful!

6.2.2015

Tanya's Diary

Screaming. You follow me from room to room screaming. All. Day. Long. I was right, I'll never poop again. Not privately anyway. I run into the bathroom and you crawl right after me with a noise decibel I'd rather not know, telling me and the neighbors what a wonderful mother I am. You climb up my legs as I sit on the toilet. My blood is hot and curdling with the screams I want to let out, but I don't think you will understand yet that I want to be LEFT ALONE! LEAVE ME ALONE!

I go to do the dishes and you do the same thing. You pull my pants down as you try to climb up my legs. Come on. Nobody wants to see that. I don't even know what I look like underneath my pants anymore. I don't have time to look in the mirror. If I did have time, I'd sit. In the quiet. And drink coffee. Maybe read a book. I imagine my hair is getting really long, but I just put it up because I don't have time to look in the mirror. If I knew I'd look good (who really cares), I'd shave my head so I had a chance of taking a quick shower.

Shower. Ahahaha.

6.16.2015

Baby Journal

Gabriel slow down! You are growing so quickly all of a sudden. You impress me every day with your patience and strength. I love SO MUCH to hear you laugh. Let's be a team and try to make everyone smile. Deal?

Dad and I go into your room to get you from your naps and you are STANDING in your crib looking out at us. It's so funny. You are very brave.

I gave you corn for the first time and boy do you like it! That's good because we love it.

God has blessed us so much Gabe. We are a strong family the three of us. I can hardly believe God loves you more than I do because Gabriel I love you SO MUCH! Like... a thousand buckets full of heavy things! That much.

- Mom

6.16.2015

Tanya's Diary

You don't seem to believe it, but I do love you. I peek into your room as you sort things out trying to fall asleep for nap. Somehow, you've learned to take your pants off and throw them out of your crib. What is this about? I'm mad so I'm going to throw my pants off! It's sad that you're so angry, but it gave me a laugh today.

I'm going to try it next time I'm mad. I imagine it will be in public. Great. I've heard prison is rough but how bad could it be. Meals cooked for me, showers, time for reading, time for fitness. It literally sounds like every dream I've had in the past six months. Day dream that is, because I haven't slept in the past six months.

7.3.2015

Baby Journal

Today as you were sitting in your high chair, we were playing peek a boo from across the room. A fly buzzed by your face and you had a near death heart attack and cried in panic. It was hilariously sad. You are my son. You should see me upon sight of a June bug. One time, your Dad found one above his head as we were driving in our old truck. He stopped at a stop sign and said "Okay, I'm going to shew a bug out the window and I don't want you to look". I cringed, closed my eyes and trusted him until he giggled and said, "Man his claws are really stuck in the headliner." So I looked and shouted, "GET IT GET IT GET IT GET IT OUT GET IT OUT." Repeating your desire does not make it happen any faster, for the record, but Gabriel... June bugs are HUGE! The thing was right above his head while he was driving. I don't understand where that bravery comes from but I don't think I was built with it.

7.3.2015

Tanya's Diary

Today is my birthday. I am 28.

Jason, Mom, Dad, my brother, and my buddy Megan remembered.

That's it.

My mother in law, and that whole side forgot me today.

It's okay, but it gives me confirmation that I don't matter. I already thought

it, so it's fine. I just had hoped it wasn't true.

7.10.2015

Baby Journal

     Hey Gabe. You are sick again and now I am sick too. Now that I have the same symptoms as you, I know what you are going through. Poor buddy. You're so tough. Even though we are sick though, we won't get today again so lets' make it great!

     Oh, I'm not positive, but I think you dance a bit now! I turned on our ABC song and you wiggled. Can't wait to dance with you Gabriel.

7.10.2015

Tanya's Diary

Your boogers move in and out as you breath and you sound like a lawn mower. I hold back my vomit as you nurse. I'm considering taking you to the doctor because I fear you may have an ear infection but I don't want to be 'that Mom' who takes their kid to the doctor for every little thing.

Jason doesn't dance with me. Please let my child enjoy dancing so we can have fun at weddings! I'm sick of staring for 3 hours into my piece of cake like it's so beautiful I just want to eat it slow and savor the flavor. No cake is that good. Cheesecake. That's a different story. But I don't think I could milk a piece of cheesecake for 3 hours. Milk a cheesecake. Hahaha. Nobody's laughing Tanya, it's just you.

7.16.2015

Baby Journal

I love to take you out to the store with us. You sit in the front of the shopping cart and look out at everything. You never fuss. I think you like it! We also put you in high chairs at restaurants now. These things were very scary to try for the first time but when we realized you could do it, oh boy! So proud of you Gabe. You and I have this noise we make together. I make it and then you make it back, and so on. It's sort of like a deep screech or deep breath. We go for a walk or run every night now. Exercise! Woohoo!

86

7.16.2015

Tanya's Diary

I don't know what I need to make me feel better. Maybe if you could say, "Hey Mommy, you're doing a great job. I know I scream a lot, but I really like the way you handled that without crying or screaming back at me. No swear words! Wow Mommy, you're amazing. What a good influence you are. Remember that oatmeal I screamed for while you were microwaving? You know, the stuff I spilled all over the floor, wall, myself, and you that has now surely turned to cement on all these surfaces? I'm sorry about that. It was nothing personal. I was just full and ready to give you a kiss because you're so wonderful and beautiful. I mean, who else can pull off that grease slicked bun on the side of your head? Last time I saw you I think it was on the top of your head. With less random strands pulled out from it. Have you been wearing that outfit for 3 days? Who knew?! You smell delightful. Sorry about those milk stains, did I do that? I didn't know that shirt had stripes! Oh, those are my boogers aren't they. See I just feel really bad about these things. I've learned my lesson and I'll never do any of these things again. Thank you. I love you. You go take a nap, I got this."

Is that so much to ask?

It is so hot outside. And the bugs here are huge. I get a sweat going from my stupid walks and then I'm hit in the eye with a horsefly. A relentless horsefly who orbits me until I scream and flail like a madwoman for all my neighbors to see. Michigan snow doesn't sound so bad.

87

7.22.2015

Baby Journal

Hey buddy. You eat little pieces of cereal all by yourself! I am excited to see what else you can do. You pick yourself up onto everything and even in the tub! Bath time is getting fun.

7.22.2015

Tanya's Diary

I don't get how I'm supposed to wash your hair and not get soap in your eyes.
Either I pour the water on your head while you're sitting up and it gets in your eyes, and
you tell me how great a mother I am. Or I lay you back and you tell the neighbors how
great a mother I am for leaning you back.

I'm thinking about getting soundproof walls installed. For my bedroom. So I
can sit in it. And cry. While you cry elsewhere. And I won't know about it. Because I
have soundproof walls. You're always crying. Maybe you see me cry every day and I'm
setting a bad example. No way, I'm a bad Mom? Just like you tell me!

I'm a Mom forever. I just want to be a wife. I want to work hard and wear my
business clothes. I want to go outside and run. And never come back. But I don't know
anyone. And the gas station down the road is pretty shady, so I won't go that far. Any
chance of escape is just a short period of time. I have to keep coming back. I'm a Mom
forever. Why do people have kids? Why did people say 'Congratulations!' when we told
them we were pregnant? If a friend of mine told me they were pregnant right now, I
would say "Ahahahaha, oh honey I'm so sorry". But I'm 1,000 miles away from all my
friends, so that won't happen. If it did, it would be over the phone, and Gabriel would be
screaming the whole time so all they would hear is 'Ahhhhhhhhh', which is pretty close
to what I would say I suppose. So there's that.

89

8.6.2015

Baby Journal

You kissed me Gabriel! Oh my heart.

8.6.2015

Tanya's Diary

You kissed me. I'm writing this down in my diary.

8.23.2015

Baby Journal

Gabriel I can't keep up anymore! You are doing so many fun things, I keep forgetting to write them down to you. Let's see… your top two teeth are coming in now, you clap, you say Ga Ga, Da Da and Hi! You make fish lips too. You hold your bottles by yourself in your bouncer seat while I work or shower and that has made life so much easier! I love to hold you but sometimes I can't. Whenever I vacuum, I have to hold you because you are very afraid of it.

8.23.2015

Tanya's Diary

You said Da Da before Ma ma. COME ON!

I see you 100% of every day, the least you could do is learn my name!

Good job on 'Hi' though. I say that one to you at least 40 times a day, it only makes sense you'd pick up on it. Hopefully you never pick up on my sarcasm though, that could come back to bite me.

I pride myself on our clean home. It is the one thing I have control over. I can keep my house clean. It helps me to destress. I'm Monica from F.R.I.E.N.D.S. I think everybody wants to be Rachel because she's hot, but I am Monica. I can't sleep with a messy house. It's kind of sad, but it makes me happy to have a clean home and I guess that's important. To know what makes me happy.

You not liking the vacuum is exhausting. Maybe I should attempt to vacuum you up so you can see the worst that could happen. Which I imagine is just … a cool hair day? And maybe ringing ears. And a lifelong fear of vacuums. Perhaps that would be a step back. Yep, moving on. Good thing I didn't write that in the baby journal.

8.29.2015

Baby Journal

You say "hi Dad" or "hi Dada" now. We took you out golfing and you waved to Dad as he was out hitting the ball. So sweet. My heart skips a beat whenever I hear your innocent baby voice. We roll a ball back and forth with you. You love it. We do too. You and Dad have this game you play every day at the dinner table. You slam your hand down onto your highchair tray and Dad moves a chair as though you are commanding it to happen.

We play for a long time and giggle. We love you so much Gabe.

I found a way to read my books as I feed you. I just read them out loud! I try to read about 1 book per month.

I volunteer at church in the infant room now. You are in the same room with me. I wanted to volunteer so I could see how other people take care of babies and see how I'm doing or what I could do better.

8.29.2015

Tanya's Diary

One book a month. AHAHAHA. Hahaha. That was a good one. I needed that.

So I volunteer now. They didn't give me much choice. They tracked me down and said I should volunteer and stood over me as I wrote my name down. I really just want to go to the service. I'm kind of bummed to be honest, but it's nice to be with you. Even more. And hear you cry. All the time. It's like I'm home. I don't know why I woke up today.

There is one lady in the infant room who says she loves volunteering in that room and can't get enough holding and squeezing the babies. She's sick. She looks normal, but what is wrong with her? If I could pay money to say I volunteered but go to Starbucks instead, I'd do it. Up to $20. $30.

Seriously, I don't know why they picked me to volunteer? I'm the one who, as soon as I drop Gabe off at the nursery, walks out the door and yells to the other Mommies waiting in line, "I'M FREE!" Then I take the only private potty break I get all week. Even if I don't have to go, I go. And I just sit there. Sometimes I come out of the bathroom and Jason is waiting there and I'm like "oh man... I'm so sick, might need a few visits to the bathroom today all by myself. What a shame." Then he catches me though with his, "Oh I guess that means you can't have Starbucks after church." What a jerk.

95

9.4.2015

Baby Journal

Wow Gabe, you are nine months old! Dad and I do yardwork and you walk around in your walker in the driveway. You are so entertained. You like to chase us and run into us.

Our great friends Rebecca and Nolan are set to have a baby boy any day now. Nolan was Dad's best friend growing up. We hope you and their son will be great friends too. His name is Marc.

9.4.2015

Tanya's Diary

It is so hard for me to show excitement to my friends. I'm trying so hard because they're so excited, and I love them. They ask for advice and I'm like... "not everyone has to have kids."

And then I can't take it back because I said it. I need to make cue card responses and keep them in my coats so I don't hurt people's feelings.

I love my Gabriel. I guess I just didn't realize how much I would be doing in this Mom job. I'm stuck. I feel like I need to quit my job. It's getting so hard to get anything done. They're constantly disappointed with me. I feel like I'm always calling back with excuses as to why I couldn't answer their calls or emails. I hate not being a loyal employee. Why are Moms the ones who have to stop working? Why me?

9.5.2015

Baby Journal

Hey buddy,

Rebecca and Nolan had their baby Marc today! We went to Georgia and visited them. They are very happy!

9.5.2015

Tanya's Diary

Rebecca went into labor in her house with us all there. It was awful. She was in so much pain. She swore and yelled at Nolan to "get the bleeping truck". He chatted with us and said very calmly, "I'll get the truck". They are hilarious. I miss them so much.

Marc was born and I cried. He's the first new baby I've held since having Gabriel. It made me realize how far we've come. He's a really cute baby. I think when you love someone, their kids are cuter to you.

They're already so chill about having a child. Why aren't they terrified? My child is older than theirs and I'm terrified every Moment! I'm terrified RIGHT NOW that Gabe will wake up because I'm writing too aggressively with this pen. Or that I'll walk by his door and my ankle will crack, waking him up. The carpet is too loud. I army crawl out of his room after I lay him down. We don't flush the toilet past 9pm anymore. We whisper at all times. I can hear my heart beat. Just when I find confidence to meander around the house while he's asleep, I step on some chatty farm toy and relearn all my animal sounds. One day, my laughing woke him up. Jason was sneaking into my office to hang with me while Gabe was asleep. He sat on a singing dog and it said, "Let's sing and play games". Jason said, "Let's not!" and kicked it across the room, into the farm toy, which educated us on our farm noises once more and somehow alerted a bumblebee that we needed help falling asleep so it started to sing us a lullaby.

9.6.2015

Baby Journal

[no entry]

9.6.2015

Tanya's Diary

Could I put Gabe in daycare throughout the day? He has such stranger anxiety and screams the whole time. I don't know anyone. Not one person. We are so scared thinking of putting him in the hands of someone we don't know to raise him from 8am to 5pm. I just checked the cost, it's $60 a day for daycare. That's $1,200 a month. We'd have to buy a second vehicle. We'd get a truck because we just have the car now, and we'd probably spend around $15,000. Add driving costs, which I don't have now because I work from home. 45 minutes to the daycare, 45 minutes home, just to sit at home and work. Then 45 minutes to pick him back up and take him back home. No increase in pay to compensate for all these increased expenses. All the while knowing my son isn't getting the love he'd get from us. I love him more than that. But I need my job. But you only get one chance to raise your children and I want to do it right. But I don't want to let Mom down and quit. I don't want to quit.

Why do people have children? I remember hearing talk about how a Mom with a few children complained she needed higher pay to cover her daycare costs and the media scolded her for having children. "You shouldn't have kids if you can't afford to take care of them", people say. People need to shut up. We're not struggling financially, but I could see how anyone else would be with this choice to make.

9.7.2015

Baby Journal

You have been getting hurt almost daily silly boy.

You got your thumb stuck in a wiffle ball, fell under water in the bathtub, and pinched your pinky in a hinge. Your cry is so desperate when you are hurt and we always run to you as soon as possible. I don't like to see you hurt buddy boy, but I know you are exploring your surroundings.

9.7.2015

Tanya's Diary

Called Mom and chatted with her. I'm so tired from crying. But she listened. She told me she wishes she could have stayed home with us kids growing up. Said she thinks about it all the time. But she had to work. I asked if it was worth it? Did she even make any money working with all the daycare costs? "No", she said. "Probably not". But the small amount she got to bring home paid for the bills and they had to pay the bills. Relatives and friends helped take care of us, for free. Because that's what family does, when they live close to each other.

This is the hardest thing I've ever done. Choosing between loving Gabe the best I can and having a job. Why can't I do both? Because I don't know anyone. If only I had a relative to help us take care of Gabe while I worked or something, maybe that would be a bit of free daycare or at least less expensive. But I don't.

I'm Tom Hanks in Castaway. I'm growing a beard. Wilson!

10.6.2015

Baby Journal

You fed yourself (very messily) with a spoon today! You imitate us with our laughing, coughing, and even the ticking of a clock. I love it so much. You make me smile. You weigh twenty pounds and are thirty inches long.

10.6.2015

Tanya's Diary

You found the bookmarks in all my books today and brought them to me. How sweet. I've read page eighty of 'The Count of Monte Cristo' about thirty times now. I wish I could say it's because I just really like that part.

Jason keeps leaving, a month here, a month there, because his unit is preparing for deployment. I never take it seriously because it's always been mentioned and then doesn't happen. My heart is ripped from one direction to another all the time. It's rough being a military spouse. It really is. If it actually happens, I don't know what I'll do. Take Gabe with me back to Michigan? Mooch off family for 9 months and live in their basement? I'd have to keep paying rent here for all our stuff in the house. I don't have time to think about it.

He called me and says he's growing a mustache with all the other guys. I have time to work on my false 'I love it' reaction.

10.13.2015

Baby Journal

So many changes with you all the time buddy boy. You say Mama, Dada, Light, and Ball.

You hand me things and give me books that you want read to you over and over. I've always dreamed of that! I love books.

I open the kitchen cupboards and find your little monkeys or crackers inside pans and Tupperware.

Dad is in California working right now. He'll be gone for about a month.

I can't believe you finally say my name Gabe.

Thank you.

10.13.2015

Tanya's Diary

It happened today. I felt it. I knew it.

Work called and said I need to put Gabe in daycare if I want to keep working. I vented to them all the things that have gone through my mind, how I don't know anyone and they cut me off. "We all did it Tanya."

"I know. But you all lived near family and friends who helped take care of your kids! You know your neighbor's name. You have a coffee shop you go to. Your barista smiles at you and knows what you want because she knows you! You have friends. You know where your hospital is. You know where the police station is. You have an emergency freaking contact!"

"We'll give you some time to think it over", they said.

"I quit", I said.

I wish Jason were here. I could really use some help.

10.16.2015

Baby Journal

[no entry]

10.16.2015

Tanya's Diary

Mom flew down to visit. She took off work just to spend time with Gabriel and me. She knows I can't sleep without Jason. She's going to slumber party in my bed with me. We had a sleepover once when my Dad went on a fishing trip years ago. We fell asleep in their big bed, watching some girly movie. I realize now that she probably wanted me to be with her. She was probably scared to be without Dad.

Mom wouldn't step on a crunchy bug, much less save us from a bad guy. But there's something about being around her. I feel safe. And cool. I'm not, but she thinks I am.

We didn't talk about work. It was nice.

Evening note added: She snores.

11.22.2015

Baby Journal

Hey buddy. Big changes lately and I can hardly keep up! This past month, we lived in a hotel in Maryland to be with Daddy while he was in a training course. We had fun. Our favorite thing to do was push the office wheelchair down the hallways of the hotel. We ate breakfast and dinner in the lobby together each day and the hotel staff loved you. They had a hard time saying goodbye to you. I had fun speaking Spanish with the cleaning ladies.

You take quite a few steps lately! You want to push everything. Your favorite thing is pushing carts at the store. Unfortunately, you throw quite a fit when you cannot push the carts so we are praying you mature past this soon so as not to make a scene in public.

We bought a house! We can move in in a few days! I am very excited to have a play room/library for you and I to play in! I'm sure it will be difficult to leave this home. We brought you home from the hospital here! Turning a new leaf. God is taking very good care of us.

11.22.2015

Tanya's Diary

It's nice to be able to give Gabe all the attention he needs, with not working now. He is happy. That's nice. I so love my Gabriel buddy. I feel really empty and without purpose though. I am happy with him one minute and then the next minute, I could stare ahead and count the seconds before my next blink. Time is heavy. I could be doing more with my time. With myself. I am meant for more than this. I hate the idea of 'stay at home Mom'. That's the last job I ever wanted. Literally. No.

We put an offer on this house nearly a year ago it seems, and our realtor called out of the blue and said we got it. What? I'd forgotten about it.

Everyone says they're so excited for us and, "Wow, how are you going to decorate it? Are you so excited? What are your paint colors?"

Why would I want to decorate a house I won't live in with my husband? Who cares? I don't care.

12.4.2015

Baby Journal

Hey buddy. You are one-year old now! Your birthday was of course December 1st, I just didn't get a chance to write to you.

We closed on our new house on your birthday. It is much bigger than our old one. Every day, we go and clean and paint to make it our own. It is a great neighborhood. A gated community even! The community has a pool! We will need to teach you how to swim, huh!

We will travel to Michigan in a few weeks to celebrate Christmas with our big family. Grandmas and grandpas, aunts and uncles, and all of your cousins too! It will be quite chilly up in Michigan this time of year so we will have to bundle you up to play outside. I'm excited to play outside with all the kiddos. Maybe there will be snow!

Christmas is a day chosen a long time ago to celebrate Jesus' birthday! People around the world buy gifts for their loved ones as a reminder of what a wonderful gift Jesus is. For Christmas, we will receive many gifts, but none of them are greater than what Jesus did for us.

You are a 'toddler' now that you can walk and climb stairs. This means you aren't a baby anymore.

I love you Gabe. Always always.

12.4.2015

Tanya's Diary

[no entry]

1.13.2016

Baby Journal

Gabriel buddy, you are having more and more fun on your own lately! You love to point out the 'ball' in every book. You love to climb the stairs. You shake your head at women to see them shake their heads too when they have dangly earrings.

You can eat yogurt all by yourself now. That probably doesn't mean anything to you but later, when you have your own baby, you will realize what an accomplishment that is.

You blow when you see a candle or if I even just say the word. And you also blow when food is hot.

You tell me "ah" when you are done with things like your milk. And you say "mo" when you don't want something.

Gabriel. I am pregnant. I found out today. Daddy and I went out to dinner tonight and I told him. We are very excited. You are a big brother! You will always be a big brother now.

This is a big responsibility, but I know you can do it. You need to make sure to set a good example for your younger sibling because they will always look up to you. Make sure you are someone to look up to, my son. I know you will be.

I love you so much buddy boy. I tell you hundreds of times a day.

-   Mom

1.13.2016

Tanya's Diary

No…

2.20.2016

Baby Journal

Gabriel buddy, you are so smart. You are learning things very quickly these days and I am very proud of you, and so is Daddy!

Daddy is in Virginia right now working. You kiss his picture goodnight and you know him very well. I am excited for you to see him again! And I'm excited to see him again too of course!

You know so many things, let me see if I can list them all...you throw things away for me when I ask, you make your bed, brush your teeth, you know the sign language for 'all done' and 'more'. You know the animal sounds for many animals like gorilla, dog, elephant, lion. You know a lot of your body parts, clock, ball, Mama, Dada, nana for banana, hi and bye bye. Gabe, I can't even note it all. You are just so smart.

I am going to school to get my certification for medical coding. I hardly have time for all the reading but I do what I can at night and during your naps. So far so good.

At night, I sing 'Jesus loves me' and I swing you all around and we both laugh. You also sit on my lap as we read books or watch VeggieTales. I love being with you my son. I hope you always love being with me.

I will always be your Mom Gabe. I'll never leave this super awesome family. And neither will Daddy. We love each other very much!

2.20.2016

Tanya's Diary

[no entry]

3.23.2016

Baby Journal

Hey buddy. Just wanted to drop you a line and let you know that whenever you hear or see Batman, you say 'nananana'. Daddy is so proud.

Your baby brother or sister seems to be growing in my belly just fine.

You point out the sun, moon, and earth nowadays. You love your bible stories and we all pray together before dinner. You hold our hands.

We did an Easter egg hunt last weekend and you did so well with the other kids! I love to take you out.

I got a job at a learning center for kids. I haven't started yet, but it is going to be great; I have hope! You get to come to work with me each day and play and learn with the other kids! I'm very excited!

3.23.2016

Tanya's Diary

[no entry]

5.8.2016

Baby Journal

Hey Gabe. Unfortunately, I had to quit my job. They had me working from 6am-6pm and I only got to see you for an hour a day to give you a bath and put you to sleep. You cried the entire time. Every minute I could hear you screaming and I could see you, afraid and sad. I cried so much every day because I was putting you through this just so I could be happy. So that I could work again. I did everything I could think of to help you get through it. I sprayed your arm with my perfume so you could smell it whenever you miss me and know I was coming back. I gave you the shirt off my back to sleep with during nap time. I guess it didn't help.

I asked to work less hours so I could have more time with you. After paying to have you in the daycare, my paycheck was enough to cover the gas I put in the truck to get there. So Daddy and I prayed about it and knew I needed to be home with you. I love you Gabe.

We traveled to Michigan to see your Aunt Jessica get married. During the long road trip, since you're potty training, we stopped a lot along the way. We felt bad for you being cooped up in a car seat the whole time so we tried to get out a good bit to stretch our legs and play.

You've been super sick ever since the day I quit my job. You had a fever of 104.3 and couldn't open your eyes they'd get so gooped shut. You coughed and screamed at me all day. You seemed like you were in a lot of pain. We took you to the doctor and you have a double ear infection. I'm sorry buddy. It will get better.

5.8.2016

Tanya's Diary

[no entry]

5.9.2016

Baby Journal

Today we went to the doctor and found out I am having a baby girl. This means you will have a little sister. Girls are different from boys and we will need to protect her and take very good care of her. I'm going to need your help with this.

Daddy will be gone until she is about four months old. He is being deployed with his work, to protect our country. He will be very far away for about 9 months, so it's just you and me.

You and I need to start a fitness routine because this is going to be tough.

You say please now. I love it. You are seventeen months old.

5.9.2016

Tanya's Diary

No…

I thought I had you figured out God. I thought surely you would cut me some slack.

You know I have everything I need to take care of a boy.

How am I supposed to do this alone?

I've seen my husband, slept in the same bed with him, for less than 30 days in the

past six months. He leaves in a couple weeks for 9 more. It doesn't even matter anymore. No

one hears my cries for help. Everyone has their own job, family, and self to take care of.

"You knew what you were getting into", they say. Did I? That makes it all okay doesn't it.

That makes it all possible. Can't I admit I was wrong? That I can't do it. I don't want this.

I don't know any of the military spouses here, but I do know that not one person I

know, has ever been without their husband for more than a week. A hunting trip, a business

trip, a men's retreat. I'm going to go into labor and what? Where does Gabe go? I drive him

to a daycare while I'm in labor? Do they have 3 day long daycare while I wait for a relative to

travel 1,000 miles south to help me for the day or two they're able to get off work? I am big

enough to admit I can't do it. Take care of Gabe, raise a new baby, clean the house, mow my

3 acre lawn weekly because if I don't the HOA will yell at me, and potty training. Oh this

potty training crap is a bunch of crap. I can't do this. I need help. Please. I don't want this.

5.26.2016

Baby Journal

[no entry]

5.26.2016

Tanya's Diary

The nurse at the counter slipped me a note. 'Are you having suicidal thoughts?'

"Yes" I nodded.

"We're keeping you overnight", she said. "It's nice up there, I think you'll like it."

You will see a lot of movies in your life. Sometimes the movies have exaggerated situations to make it more exciting to watch. I found out that a Psychiatric Ward is a real thing. You really do write with crayons because anything else could be used as a weapon. There are no toilet seats. No mirrors. That one I was cool with. You return your soap and toothpaste when you're done with it in the allotted time. You eat supervised and your tray is reviewed after you're finished to make sure you didn't steal the plastic knife. You have group therapy sessions, make crafts, and talk with other people with problems far worse than your own. You're scared.

But for me… I was happy. Because there were no children. No whining. No screaming in my face, or throwing of food, or four hundred messes to clean up. No snack snack Snack SNACKS! No potty accidents everywhere all the time on everything! No one calling me Mama!

1.13.2017

Baby Journal

Kara.

That is your name.

We picked your name on our Christmas road trip to Michigan a few years ago.

You were born on September 13th. That is your Daddy and my anniversary! Our eight-year wedding anniversary surprise. We planned to go out for seafood that night to celebrate. But you came in the middle of the night. A surprise natural, unmedicated birth even though I had a scheduled c-section. You were very anxious to enter the world! You were six pounds, five ounces, and nineteen inches long.

I call you Carebear.

You are so beautiful.

You are everything I always dreamed having a baby would be like. You are snuggly, soft, you enjoy baths, you fall asleep in my arms and in the curve of my neck. Gabriel loves you and is so helpful. You are both my pride and joy. During Gabriel buddy's naptime, you fall right asleep in my arms and I just hold you. I know I won't get a thing done, but oh I love you Kara.

You are my gift I do not deserve.

If you and your husband decide to have children one day, I will help you any time I can. I promise. And if you decide not to have children, that's fine too. Being a Mom is really hard.

1.13.2017

Tanya's Diary

It is amazing the things we get through. I've made it through 100% of my worst days. I thank God that someone finally listened to me. It was Jason. He found me with the gun. He said he was sorry, but he had to take me to the hospital. "Good", I said. " I want to do what's right for us. I want to be a good Mom". I just thought I'd get some magic potion happy pills. I heard about them on a commercial.

It was amazing, being there. I think I'll make it an annual thing. Just kidding self. You're so funny. But it was relieving. Time away. And they listened to me.

"I'm not deploying", he said. "They're not making me go."

I got my tubes tied. That was an easy decision. I laughed when they asked if I wanted the procedure. They didn't appreciate my humor at the hospital. I thought it was a rhetorical question.

Like... would you like an extra shot of espresso?

Does a bear poop in the woods?

39202253R00078

Made in the USA
Middletown, DE
16 March 2019